beetle bailey

TAKE TEN

by mort walker

TOR
A TOM DOHERTY ASSOCIATES BOOK

ISBN: 812-56094-9

A Tom Doherty Associates Original

Printed in the United States of America

beetle bailey

TAKE TEN

"THE LAST STRAW"
GOOFING OFF AGAIN, BEETLE. THIS IS THE LAST STRAW!!

NOW YOU STAND RIGHT THERE TILL I CAN THINK OF THE BEST WAY TO PUNISH YOU!

POW!

AW, THE HECK WITH IT! LET'S GO GET A SODA
NOW WHERE DID HE RUN OFF TO?!
END

LT. FUZZ FLIPS
DON'T FORGET! I OUTRANK YOU! I'M THE BOSS AND YOU'RE NOTHING!

AT SARGE
ONE -- TWO -- THREE

I'D BETTER TELL THE CAPTAIN ABOUT THIS

BUT, SIR. AREN'T YOU GOING TO COME OUT AND STEP BETWEEN SARGE AND LT. FUZZ?
OH, LET THEM WORK OUT THEIR OWN PROBLEM

BUT LT. FUZZ IS RIDING SARGE TOO FAR! HE DOESN'T KNOW WHAT HE'S GETTING INTO
THAT'S THE REASON I'M NOT GOING OUT THERE
WHY'S THAT, SIR?

I **KNOW** WHAT I'D BE GETTING INTO

YOU'D LIKE TO **HIT** ME WOULDN'T YOU?

YOU KNOW THE PENALTY FOR HITTING A COMMISSIONED OFFICER, DON'T YOU?
YOU'D GET COURT MARTIALED - THAT'S WHAT!!

PROBABLY SIX MONTHS IN THE STOCKADE AND LOSS OF STRIPES

SO YOU'D BETTER GET THAT IDEA OUT OF YOUR HEAD

I GUESS I TOLD **HIM!**

THERE MUST BE SOMETHING ABOUT **WISHING** AN OFFICER WOULD SLIP AND BREAK HIS NECK!
ARMY REGULATI
VOL
10

END

"SPEAKING
POST EXCHANGE
NEW!
49¢
TRY IT!

UP"
LET'S SEE -- I WANT A RAZOR AND SOME BLADES AND --

PARDON ME, I WANT A TOOTHBRUSH, PLEASE

STOP BUCKING THE LINE, STUPID! WHO DO YOU THINK YOU ARE?

GULP!

I THINK I'M GENERAL HALFTRACK
US

I DON'T CARE IF YOU **ARE** A GENERAL! I WAS HERE **FIRST!**
NEW!
49¢
TRY IT!

YOU MEAN YOU'RE NOT SORE, SIR?
OF COURSE NOT! IT WAS SPIRIT LIKE YOURS THAT MADE THIS COUNTRY GREAT!
US

HEH! HEH! I LIKE YOUR SPIRIT, BOY! MORE PEOPLE SHOULD STAND UP FOR THEIR RIGHTS

IN THAT CASE, THERE'S SOME-THING I'D LIKE TO SAY ABOUT ARMY FOOD!
I THINK I MADE A BIG MISTAKE

AND HOW ABOUT A 40-HOUR WEEK!
GENERAL'S OFFICE

YOU'RE BEGINNING TO MAKE A PEST OF YOURSELF!
LIBERTY WAS NEVER WON EASILY
US

I DIDN'T FINISH SPEAKING TO YOU ABOUT A RAISE IN PAY!

WE AMERICANS WILL NEVER STOP FIGHTING FOR OUR FREEDOMS!

THINK OF IT THIS WAY-- I'M JUST STANDING UP FOR MY RIGHTS!

STOCKADE
END

"The
SCIENTIFIC

SHIRKER"
LET'S SEE --- TODAY'S THE 22ND, TEN O'CLOCK --- AND SARGE IS ON HIS WAY TO THE SUPPLY ROOM
WHAT ARE YOU WRITING, BEETLE?

EVERYTHING IS SO SCIENTIFIC THESE DAYS --WHY NOT BE SCIENTIFIC ABOUT GOOFING OFF!

IS THAT WHAT ALL THOSE FIGURES ARE?

I'VE BEEN WORKING ON THEM A WEEK
GOLLY!

IN JUST A MINUTE I'LL BE READY TO SNEAK OVER TO THE P.X.
I'LL GO WITH YOU

GOT OUR ROUTE FIGURED OUT YET, BEETLE?

WE SNEAK OUT THE BACK DOOR. SARGE CAUGHT US HERE TWO TIMES. BY LAW OF AVERAGES IT'S SAFE

YEAH ... LET'S GO!

WE WERE SPOTTED GOING THIS WAY THREE TIMES, SO OUR ODDS ARE VERY GOOD

HE CAUGHT US ALONG HERE **ONCE**. I FIGURE IT'S A 50-50 CHANCE WE GOTTA TAKE

BY LAW OF AVERAGES, THIS IS THE BEST ROAD TO TAKE FOUR TO ONE

SEE! WHAT DID I TELL YOU?-- WE MADE IT!
YOU'RE A GENIUS!
PX

WELL, BACK TO THE OLD CALCULATIONS

END

"DELAYED
SARGE, THE GENERAL WILL BE BY TO INSPECT IN TEN MINUTES!

ACTION"
YES, SIR

Z

SARGE, DIDN'T YOU HEAR ME?
YES, SIR

WELL, DON'T YOU THINK YOU'D BETTER GET BUSY?

I GUESS I'D BETTER GET STARTED ON MY NAP SO I'LL HAVE TIME TO CLEAN UP WHEN I HEAR HIM COMING

DON'T WORRY, SIR. I'LL GET THE OFFICE STRAIGHT BEFORE THE GENERAL GETS HERE
WHY DO YOU ALWAYS WAIT TILL THE **LAST MINUTE!**

THE TROUBLE IS HE NEVER EVEN STARTS TILL HE HEARS SOMEONE YELL, "THE GENERAL IS HERE!"
HMMM

WOULD YOU LIKE TO HELP PLAY A TRICK ON SARGE?
YOU BET, SIR!

THE GENERAL IS HERE!!

THE GENERAL IS HERE!!
SLAM

THE GENERAL IS HERE!!
BEETLE! I MIGHT HAVE KNOWN!

I'LL TEACH HIM!

GENERAL!!
IT'S YOU!!

YOU WERE EXPECTING A TICKER-TAPE PARADE MAYBE?
END

"The CRUMMY CONNECTION"
WHEN YOU'VE FINISHED WITH THAT, GET MY PHONE LINE CONNECTED, SERGEANT
YES, SIR

CONNECTING A PHONE LINE ISN'T A DIFFICULT JOB. ANY DUMB-BELL COULD DO IT

IN THAT CASE I'LL TELL BEETLE TO DO IT

ISN'T THAT PHONE LINE CONNECTED YET, SARGE?
I'LL SEE, SIR

☆⁞⁞@☆#6 HAVEN'T YOU EVEN **STARTED** TO LAY DOWN THAT PHONE LINE, BEETLE ?

ONE THING YOU CAN ALWAYS COUNT ON WHEN YOU GIVE BEETLE A JOB TO DO
YOU HAVE TO DOUBLE CHECK TO SEE IF HE'S DOING IT!

FIRST I HAVE TO READ UP ON HOW TO DO IT
PHONE MANUAL

YOU'VE CONNECTED PHONE LINES BEFORE!

NOW GET BUSY!
OKAY, SARGE

HAVE IT YOUR WAY

COMICS

WHO LAID THIS PHONE LINE?
BEETLE, SIR. IS ANYTHING WRONG?

I CAN'T GET ANY ANSWER. GO CHECK THE LINE AND SEE WHAT THE TROUBLE IS!
YES, SIR

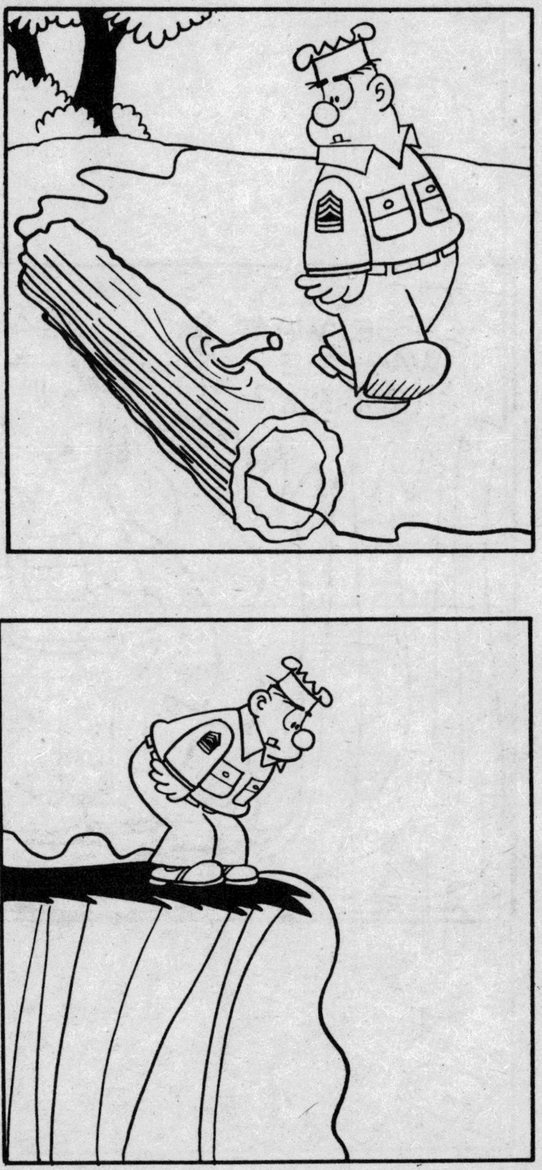

OH, HELLO, SARGE. WHAT WAS THE TROUBLE?

WOULD YOU LIKE A LIST, SIR? OR DO YOU WANT TO SEE IT IN PERSON?
END

The PHONEY
KILLER, HAVE YOU SEEN SARGE?
US

PATROL
HE LEFT WITH BEETLE ON A SCOUTING MISSION EARLY THIS MORNING, SIR

I TOLD HIM PLAINLY THAT SCOUTING MISSION WAS **TOMORROW!**
US

AND LOOK! HE EVEN FORGOT HIS RIFLE
US
US

AND THE MISSION SHOULDN'T TAKE MORE THAN AN HOUR! HE'S BEEN GONE ALL DAY!

HE'LL PROBABLY HAVE A BEAUTIFUL EXCUSE-- BUT I WON'T FALL FOR IT!
US

IT WAS A BEAUTIFUL RECONNAISSANCE JOB IF I DO SAY SO MYSELF, SIR

I BEGAN BY WADING UPSTREAM SO WE WOULDN'T LEAVE A TRAIL
FIRST, HE FELL IN THE CREEK

WHEW! WHAT A STUPID, FOULED-UP PATROL THAT WAS!

THEN I CIRCLED THE ENEMY OUTPOST AND APPROACHED FROM THE REAR
I'LL BET WE WANDERED AROUND LOST IN THOSE WOODS TWO HOURS

I GOT AN INTELLIGENCE REPORT THAT THE ENEMY HAD MOVED TO HIGHER GROUND
A KID SAID HE SAW SOME SOLDIERS CLIMBING A HILL

I GOT THE DRAW ON THEM AND THEY GAVE UP WITH-OUT A STRUGGLE

I INFILTRATED THEIR DEFENSES
WHILE WE WERE SITTING DOWN RESTING THEY CAME RIGHT PAST US!

WE DREW STRAWS TO SEE WHICH SIDE GOT CREDIT FOR THE CAPTURE

HE'LL PROBABLY TRY TO MAKE A GOOD STORY, BUT THE CAPTAIN'S TOO SMART TO FALL FOR IT

CONGRATULATIONS!
END

Sarge's Robots
AWRIGHT!! WAKE UP! HUP! TWO! THREE!

I CAN'T WORK TODAY, SARGE! I HAVE A SORE BACK

SOLDIERS DON'T **HAVE** SORE BACKS! GET BUSY! HUP! TWO! THREE!

BRUSH TEETH! HUP! TWO! THREE!

SARGE HAS NO RESPECT FOR INDIVIDUALITY! HE WANTS US ALL TO BE ROBOTS!
LET'S SHOW HIM HOW AWFUL IT WOULD BE IF WE DID BECOME MECHANICAL MEN!

OKAY, YOU GUYS! FALL OUT FOR--- OH, THEY'RE ALREADY COMING OUT

THE GROUNDS ARE DIRTY, SO BEFORE BREAKFAST YOU MUST --
POLICE-- AREA

NOW YOU CAN--
EAT--- BREAKFAST!

WELL, HOW ARE THE MEN THIS MORNING, SARGE?

INSPECTION WILL BE AT TEN, SO--
GO..
TO..
WORK!

NOT BAD, SIR. OF COURSE THEY STILL NEED MORE DISCIPLINE, BUT THEY'RE IMPROVING
END

"ALWAYS
WHERE IN BLAZES HAVE YOU BEEN, BEETLE?

UNRELIABLE"
AT THE MOVIES, WHY?

WE HAD A PING PONG GAME SCHEDULED AT SIX
I THOUGHT THAT WAS TOMORROW
TODAY, YOU IDIOT! I WAITED TWO HOURS FOR YOU!!

I CAN'T DEPEND ON YOU FOR ANYTHING
BOY! WHAT A SORE-HEAD

IMAGINE MAKING A BIG FUSS OVER SUCH A LITTLE THING!

GEE WHIZ! I JUST FORGOT!

THE NEXT JOB THAT COMES UP **HE'S** GETTING!

BETTER GET SOMEONE TO WAKE YOU FOR THE EARLY BRIEFING, SARGE
YES, SIR

BEETLE, I HAVE TO BE UP AT 5:30 SHARP! I'M GIVING YOU THE JOB TO WAKE ME!
OKAY, SARGE, DON'T WORRY, YOU'LL BE UP IN TIME

I'D BETTER BE UP ON TIME OR I'LL **MURDER** HIM!

THE MORE I THINK ABOUT IT, THE MORE I WISH I'D TOLD SOMEONE ELSE TO WAKE ME! I DON'T TRUST HIM!

NOW I CAN'T SLEEP FROM WORRYING THAT HE WON'T DO HIS JOB!

I CAN'T TAKE THE CHANCE. IT'S NEARLY TIME ANYWAY

I KNEW IT! IT'S 5:30 AND LOOK AT HIM SNORING AWAY!
BEETLE!

SEE, SARGE. I TOLD YOU YOU'D BE UP!
END

"The HUNGRY COOK"

CHIPPED BEEF ON TOAST, SHREDDED CARROTS WITH RAISINS, AND LEMON PUDDING

BLAAH! I WOULDN'T FEED THAT STUFF TO A DOG. I'M GOING TO EAT AT THE P.X.!

JUST A MINUTE, BEETLE. COME BACK HERE!

YEAH, WHAT DO YOU WANT?

UH--WOULD YOU BRING ME BACK 2 HAMBURGERS AND A CHOCOLATE MILKSHAKE?
END

"Food Patrol"
HURRY UP, SARGE. YOU'RE THE LAST ONE TO FINISH EATING AGAIN
IT'S NOT HEALTHY TO EAT FAST!

OF ALL PEOPLE COOKIE SHOULD KNOW THAT

I WAS PLANNING ON DOING SOME WORK TONIGHT BUT I'D BETTER LET THAT BIG MEAL DIGEST FIRST

I BETTER HAVE A LITTLE SNACK BEFORE I GO TO BED

SARGE HAS WORN A PATH BETWEEN THE MESS HALL AND THE OFFICE

SEEMS LIKE I WAS BUSY ALL DAY BUT I DIDN'T GET MUCH DONE

THE TROUBLE IS I CAN'T GET STARTED IN THE MORNING WITHOUT A BIG HEARTY BREAKFAST

BUT IT ALWAYS MAKES ME LATE GETTING INTO THE OFFICE

THEN AT TEN I HAVE TO RETURN TO THE MESS HALL FOR COFFEE

I BARELY GET A HALF HOUR'S WORK DONE BEFORE LUNCHTIME

THEN IT'S OUT TO COFFEE AT THREE AND BACK AGAIN FOR SUPPER AT **FIVE**

NO WONDER I GET NOTHING DONE

THIS IS TERRIBLE! I'LL JUST HAVE TO STOP ALL THIS RUNNING BACK AND FORTH TO THE MESS HALL!

END

The TASTY VICTORY
with GENERAL HALFTRACK
I HOPE YOU MEN ARE ON YOUR TOES WHEN THE GENERAL CALLS FOR THE ATTACK TONIGHT
DO WE HAVE TO GO THROUGH THAT AGAIN?

WHY DOES HE MAKE SUCH A BIG DEAL OUT OF EVERYTHING?

YOU DON'T SEEM TO REALIZE HOW IMPORTANT THIS IS TO HIM

HE'S BEEN WORKING ON HIS NEW PLAN OF ATTACK ALL DAY

I'VE GOT THE ENTIRE OPERATION PLOTTED ON THE MAP WITH THE ROUTES OF ADVANCE

LOOK AT HIM! HE CAN TASTE THE VICTORY NOW!

THEY WON'T GET BY OUR DEFENSE TONIGHT, SIR!

THE RECONNAISSANCE PLANE HAS SPOTTED THEM, SIR!
GOOD!

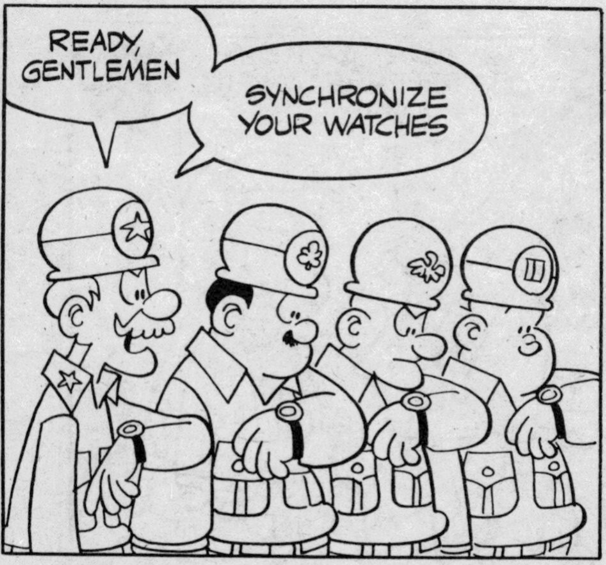
READY, GENTLEMEN
SYNCHRONIZE YOUR WATCHES

GET THOSE SCOUTS OUT WITH THE RADAR AND WALKIE-TALKIE
YES, SIR

GO!

IT'S GOING LIKE CLOCK-WORK, SIR
HA! I KNEW IT WOULD

JUST SHOWS WHAT A LITTLE TOP LEVEL THINKING CAN DO!

THE ADVANCE SCOUTS REPORT MOVEMENT ON THE SOUTH ROAD, SIR!
TELL PERIMETER GUARDS TO PUT UP THE ROAD BLOCK!

OKAY! LET'S **MOVE IN!**

ICE
CREAM

WHAT FLAVOR DO YOU WANT, GENERAL?
END

IRONSIDES
WHUMP!
?

STOP! YOU DROPPED SOMETHING!

HE DIDN'T HEAR ME!
NO LABELS ON THE CRATE! I WONDER WHAT'S INSIDE!

WELL, THERE'S ONE SURE WAY TO FIND OUT!

?!!? FOR GOSH SAKE!

A MINI-TANK!

WHAT WON'T THEY THINK UP NEXT?

IT'S A LITTLE SNUG BUT I ACTUALLY FIT INSIDE.
HOW ABOUT THAT?

OH, OH!
I'M STUCK!

COOKIE! HELP ME!
NOW WHAT?

DO SOMETHING! I'M STUCK IN HERE!
?

I'VE RUINED THREE CAN-OPENERS! MAYBE IF I SMEAR YOU WITH LARD YOU'LL SLIDE OUT!
NO!
NO!
NO!

STAGE DOOR
YOU'RE STUCK?
COSTUMES

TRY THE DOC! HE HAS A STOMACH PUMP, SARGE!
HAR! HAR!

YEAH! **DO SOMETHING**, BEETLE, BEFORE THE WHOLE CAMP FINDS OUT ABOUT IT!

I'M NOT SO SURE I LIKE THIS IDEA, BEETLE!

BUT, SARGE, THIS CAMP SHOW COSTUME IS A PERFECT DISGUISE. THIS HOOP SKIRT COVERS UP THE WHOLE TANK!
COSTUMES

I WISH BEETLE HADN'T PUT THIS LIPSTICK ON ME. I FEEL LIKE SUCH A FOOL!

LOOK! THE MINI-TANK'S TRACKS GO INTO THOSE BUSHES!
WE MUST BE GETTING CLOSE, SIR!

I'LL HIDE IN HERE TILL I FIGURE OUT MY NEXT MOVE!

YIPE!

HELLO, BOYS! ARE YOU LOOKING FOR BLUE-BERRIES TOO?

NO, MADAM, WE'RE LOOKING FOR AN X14 QT SMALL TANK. DID YOU HAPPEN TO SEE ONE PASS BY THIS WAY?
SILLY BOY

YAAHHHH!
YOU SCARED US, LADY!
SCREETCH!

I WOULDN'T KNOW THE DIFFERENCE BETWEEN AN X14 QT SMALL TANK AND A UHIB HELICOPTER.
?

AFTER HER! SHE KNOW
MORE THAN SHE SAYS
GOLLY! SHE CAN RUN FAST!

DOGGONE IT! I GAVE MYSELF AWAY!

HOLY COW!! THEY MEAN BUSINESS!
BANG! BANG! BANG!

CRASH!
I'M DONE FOR!

GOSH! I NEVER THOUGHT THIS SILLY COSTUME WOULD SAVE MY LIFE!

REALLY? YOU ALMOST GOT KILLED TODAY, SARGE?
YEAH, BUT SOMEHOW EVERYTHING WORKED OUT HAPPILY!

THE ARMY FOUND THEIR MINI-TANK AND YOU GUYS GOT **ME** BACK!
U.S.
The END